Thomas Readett

Art Gallery of South Australia • Adelaide

Acknowledgement of Country

Jack Buckskin of Kuma Kaaru

AGSArlu tampinthi ngadlu Kaurna yartangka tikanthi, ngadlu tampinthi kumartarna Yaitya Miyurna Tarnanthi-itya warpulayinthi.

Jack Kanya Buckskinrlu, Kuma Kaaru Cultural Services-ityanungku ngadlulitya warpulayinthi, Warra Kaurna ngutu-atpanthi ngadlu tirkatitya.

AGSA acknowledges that we are on Kaurna land and acknowledges all other Aboriginal and Torres Strait Islander peoples working with Tarnanthi.

Jack Kanya Buckskin from Kuma Kaaru Cultural Services is working with us and teaching us language.

Trudy Inkamala, Arrernte/Luritja people, Northern Territory, born Hamilton Downs Station, Northern Territory 1940, Roxanne Petrick, Alyawarr/eastern Arrernte people, Northern Territory, born Mparntwe (Alice Springs), Northern Territory 1986, Dulcie Raggett, Luritja people, Northern Territory, born Mparntwe (Alice Springs), Northern Territory 1970, Marlene Rubuntja, Arrernte people, Northern Territory, born Mparntwe (Alice Springs), Northern Territory 1961, Rosabella Ryder, Arrernte people, Northern Territory, born Mparntwe (Alice Springs), Northern Territory 1975, Dulcie Sharpe, Luritja people, Northern Territory, born Hamilton Downs Station, Northern Territory 1957, Rhonda Sharpe, Luritja people, Northern Territory, born Mparntwe (Alice Springs), Northern Territory 1977, Roxanne Sharpe, Luritja people, Northern Territory, born Mparntwe (Alice Springs), Northern Territory 1985, Valerie Stafford, Anmatyerre people, Northern Territory, born Coniston Station, Northern Territory 1963, *Every face has a story, every story has a face: Kulila!*, 2016, Mparntwe (Alice Springs), Northern Territory, mixed media, dyed blankets, polyester wadding, embroidery thread, twigs, 228.0 x 120.0 x 100.0 cm (overall); Acquisition through Tarnanthi Festival of Contemporary Aboriginal & Torres Strait Islander Art supported by BHP 2017
photo: Saul Steed

inside cover: John Prince Siddon, Walmajarri people, Western Australia, born Derby, Western Australia 1964, *Mixed Up Wallpaper #3*, 2020, Fitzroy Crosing, Western Australia Courtesy Fremantle Arts Centre

Jack has provided us with some key Kaurna words relating to art to help us navigate the contents of this book!

Tarnanthi means to come forth or appear – like the sun and the first emergence of light

Tura Wirkalirkala is a painter

Tirkanthi is learning

Tura is a picture

Pintyalintyala is a creator

Piipa is a book

Kurdanyi is a rainbow or a colour

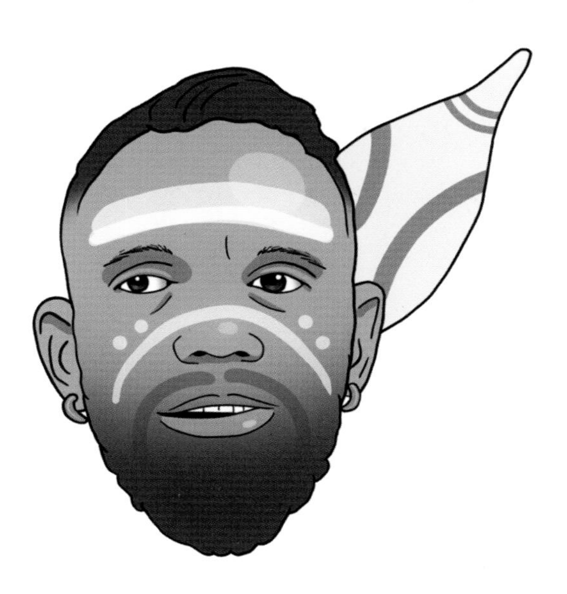

How to use this book

Welcome to the *Make and Create* book. This book is full of ideas and activities, inspired by some of the world's leading Aboriginal and Torres Strait Islander contemporary artists. Each artist has a different activity for you to explore, either on your own or with a friend. Try some painting, printmaking, drawing, collage and sculpting inspired by the artists featured in this book. This book will help you to look at works of art in a way that brings you and the artist closer together.

My name is Thomas Readett, I am a Ngarrindjeri man and artist from Kaurna Country, South Australia. I work as a member of the Tarnanthi Education Team at the Art Gallery of South Australia, the place where I am creating this book.

Tarnanthi is a celebration of Aboriginal and Torres Strait Islander art from across the country.

From when I was young I have always loved making art; making art makes us feel great and makes us happier. Exploring different types of art and different techniques builds our skills and confidence. In bringing you this book, I have been very lucky to work with some of the best artists in the country.

The artists featured here all create works of art in various ways and their activities will help you to understand art in a different way and help you to develop your own artistic style and your own thoughts about art.

The artists in this book have all been asked the following questions in order to give some insight into why they became artists and why they do what they do:

- What made you become an artist?
- How would you describe your work?
- What is the role of an artist?
- What do you enjoy about making art?
- Who inspired you?

Welcome to Country by Jack Buckskin
at Tarnanthi launch, 2018
photo: Nat Rogers

John Prince Siddon

Walmajarri people, Western Australia
born Derby, Western Australia, 1964

Biography

John Prince Siddon, a Walmajarri artist, was born in 1964 in Derby, Western Australia, and now lives in Fitzroy Crossing, in northwest Western Australia. He works with one of Australia's most experimental art centres – Mangkaja Arts, where his father, the artist Pompey Siddon, was one of the art centre's founding painters. When younger, Prince worked on cattle stations, but after a horse-riding accident he was unable to continue this type of work, taking up painting at Mangkaja Arts in 2009. His painting style is known for being quirky and for considering both subject matter and pattern-making in the execution of his works. His practice extends beyond painting to include sculpture and installation, including the carving of boab nuts and painting on various 3D materials.

Prince often paints about local and global events, notably the 2020 bushfires on Kangaroo Island in South Australia. His imagery of these incidents is combined with the ancestral stories of his desert homeland to create scenes with patterns and dazzling spectrums of colour.

What made you become an artist?

After an accident I wasn't able to work as a stockman any more. I had so many ideas and I was bored, so I started to paint all kinds of things to pass the time. Now once I started I just couldn't stop.

How would you describe your work?

Well to me, I'm still mixing stories, painting them better than one, somebody has to do it.

As Burke and Wills, what true Aussies. I am making my own stories and making them fit altogether. I'm trying to piece together every animal – North, South, East West – trying to mix them up like a jigsaw – they love each other, they hate each other. Landscape, dreamtime stories, kids' paintings, poetry, animals; put them all together, it's all the same with my paintings.

What is the role of an artist?

I see that art is always a part of my life and it's really important for me to tell my stories this way, get them out and share them with the world. If I can say what I want to say, I can say it through my art and that can help change people's ideas about art that is made in remote communities.

What do you enjoy about making art?

There are no rules and it helps me get out all my worries. I get worried watching the news and thinking about what is going on in the world and what is happening in my community all around me. I feel sad and get stressed out – art is a way for me to deal with these issues and communicate with the outside world.

Who inspired you?

These kind people and animals and the things are my true blue heroes, not the ones you see on the movies, local hero make you think twice sometimes, make you cry, laugh most of the stories are true. It's not about getting a top model or the brave things they have done. It's who you are as a person or animals they deserve to be who they once was many untold stories out there today.

John Prince Siddon, Walmajarri people, Western Australia, born Derby, Western Australia 1964, *Fear*, 2019, Fitzroy Crossing, Western Australia, synthetic polymer paint on canvas, 120.0 x 120.0 cm; Acquisition through Tarnanthi: Festival of Contemporary Aboriginal & Torres Strait Islander Art supported by BHP 2020 © John Prince Siddon/Mangkaja Arts Resource Agency

John Prince Siddon, Walmajarri people, Western Australia, born Derby, Western Australia 1964, *Mix it all up*, 2019, Fitzroy Crossing, Western Australia, synthetic polymer paint on canvas, 120.0 x 240.0 cm; Acquisition through Tarnanthi: Festival of Contemporary Aboriginal & Torres Strait Islander Art supported by BHP 2020

Activity

Boab nut design

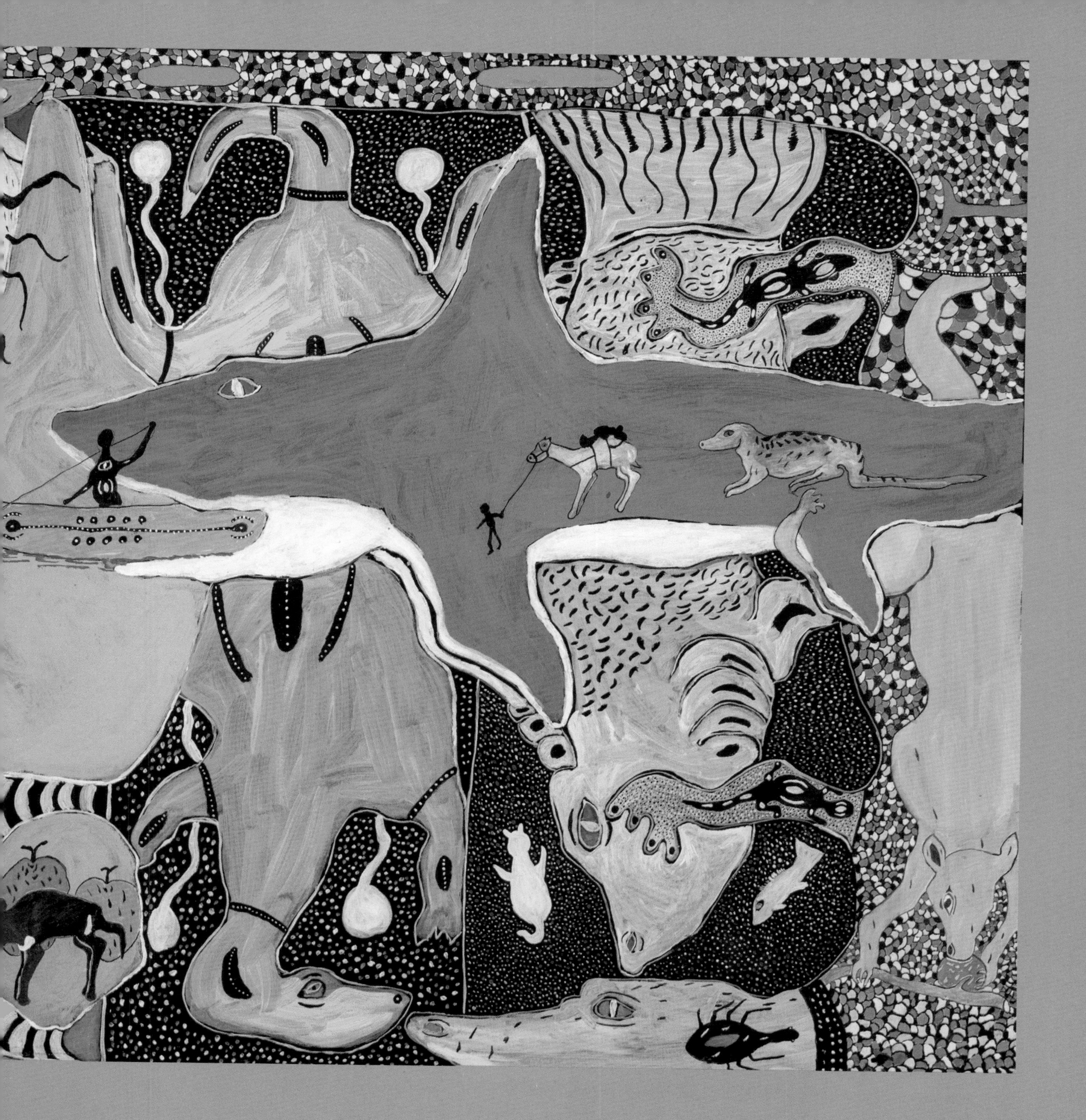

Materials
Card, pastels and scissors

Level
Easy

People
One or many

Step 1

Select colours from nature and a favourite animal.

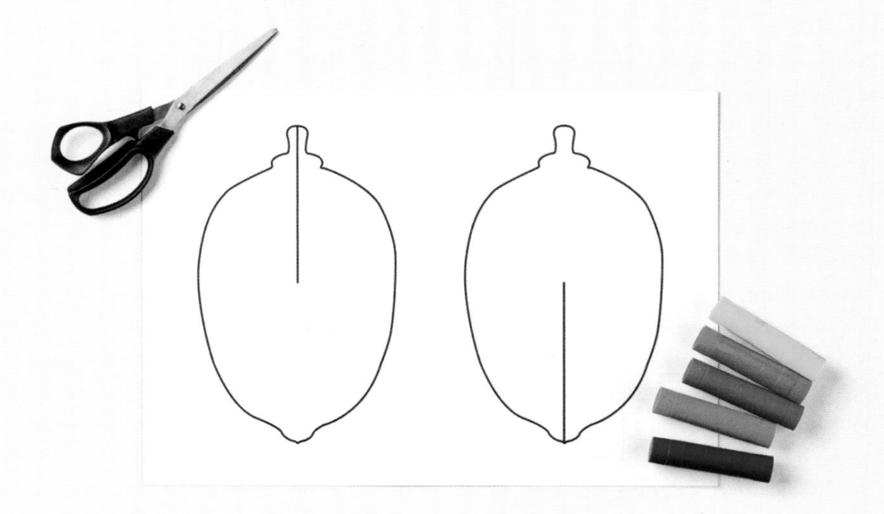

I'm going to use the outline of a horse and the pattern of a zebra! The patterns I have picked from nature are leaves and bubbles because I love forests and water.

Tip

Think about shapes from either and use these for positive or negative shapes.

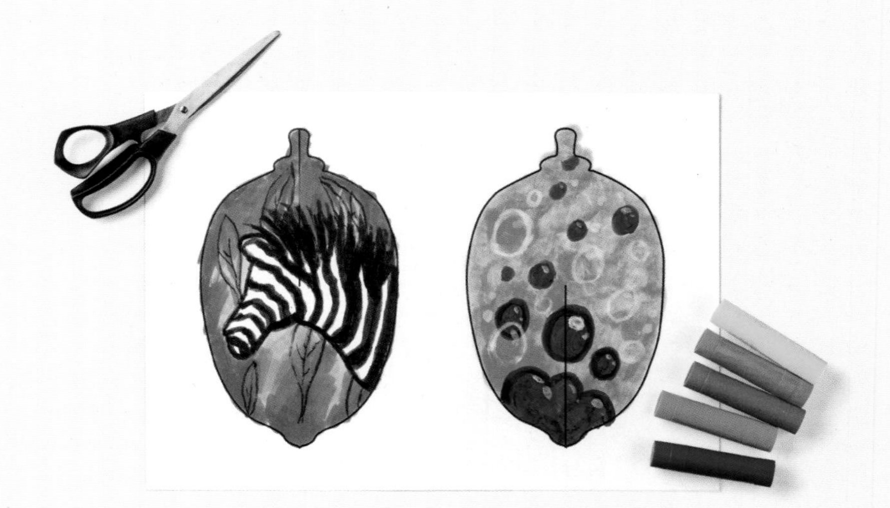

Step 2

Draw your designs, you can be completely random with these. I am using Colour Slicks but you can use pencils or textas too!

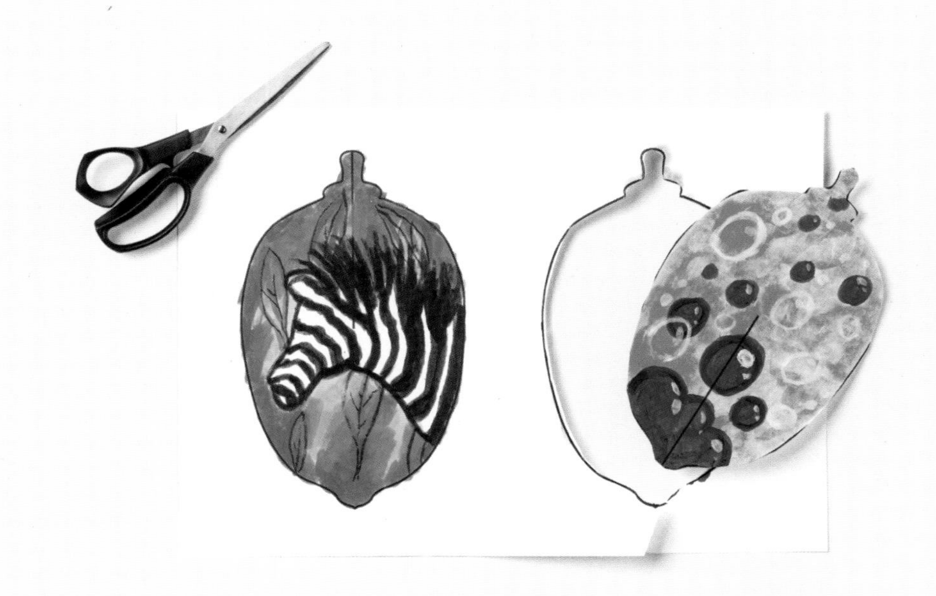

Step 3

Cut out your designs and slot them into one another and your Boab nut is complete!

Elizabeth Yanyi Close

Pitjantjatjara / Yankunytjatjara people, South Australia
born Adelaide 1986

Biography

Elizabeth Yanyi Close is a Pitjantjatjara/Yankunytjatjara artist currently working in Adelaide. She began painting in 2007 while also working as a registered nurse in hospital emergency departments. She began her career as a full-time artist in 2016. Although she paints on canvas, she is best known for her large-scale public works of art. Her pieces are bold and immersive and include a vibrant palette, strong lines and patterns.

Much like the murals made by the Mexican muralists in the 1930s, Close brings art to, and shares its declarative power with, the masses through her contemporary murals. These monumental works of art highlight the importance of placemaking and assert Aboriginal culture within the wider community. Her murals are avenues whereby Close not only shares her ancestry and her connection to Country, but also that of Aboriginal people across Australia. In addition, she invites the viewer to consider their connection and belonging to a place.

Close works individually but has also collaborated with other artists on murals across Adelaide and in Australia and Europe.

What made you become an artist?

I have always been creative and spent much time as a small child drawing and painting with my grandmother, who was also very creative. During my schooling and for some time after, I didn't engage with art much. I returned to the visual arts when my grandmother passed away when I was aged twenty-two. I was overwhelmed with grief at the loss of my strongest connection to my A̱ngu culture and I needed to process that. Around 2009 I returned to the thing she and I had shared and began to paint again. But I soon discovered what a powerful conduit art can be to culture. It gave me the ability to connect with my grandmother through those stories. What started out as a therapeutic tool and a hobby soon flourished into a part-time arts practice, and by 2016 I was ready to step into a full-time arts practice, which is where I am today.

How would you describe your work?

My work is a bold and vibrant fusion of expression and storytelling. I use a vivid palette to express my connection to Country. I work primarily in 2D, but I am constantly innovating, in both my studio practice and my public arts practice.

What is the role of an artist?

I think artists have many roles. I think we inspire and surprise, and evoke emotion, but fundamentally I believe that the artist's role is to provoke thought and discussion. The role of the artist working in the public space is amplified somewhat because it takes place outside artistic circles, which can be limited. Public art takes paintings out of the galleries and places it in the public realm for everyone to enjoy and be challenged by.

I see my role within public art as increasing the visibility of Aboriginal arts and culture. Aboriginal art on a large scale enriches the public space and more broadly reflects an Australia that I would like to live in – one in which all cultures are valued. This is what drives me to create.

detail: Elizabeth Close, Pitjantjatjara/ Yankunytjatjara people, South Australia, born Adelaide 1986, *Goodwood Station*, collaborative mural with Shane Cook and Thomas Readett, 2020, Adelaide, exterior acrylic, dimensions variable

photo: Amber Eyes Imagery

What do you enjoy about making art?

I enjoy creating works that have a strong aesthetic and deep meaning. I enjoy the ability to experiment and take risks, even if that means there are works that are disasters. I learn from each and every work that goes wrong and I take that forward into the next one. Without risk, there is no evolution. I love that sudden rush of inspiration, where I sit bolt upright because I have something new I want to try – writing myself a note at 3 am because I know I'll have forgotten my idea by morning. But one of the things I value most about being an artist is the ability to collaborate with others. Elements of it come from relationships with galleries, institutions and organisations, but most importantly it comes from relationships with other artists. Collaboration has been a huge part of my arts practice; I learn something new every time I work with another artist, be it technique, medium, themes or ideas.

Through relationships, comes opportunity.

Who inspired you?

The strong Aboriginal women who came before me inspire me. My Kami – my grandmother – who passed away, and my many extended Kami still living and creating at home on Country – and Aboriginal women artists more broadly. They work incredibly hard, and it is their ground-breaking work for decades that has fostered an environment where Aboriginal art is valued. I am inspired by my Tjamu for his cultural strength and the way he has passed down Aṉangu *tjukurpa* and cultural knowledge to the next generations. I am inspired by so many other artists, some of whom I have been lucky enough to work with and learn from, particularly in the public space. It was the experience of creating a five-storey mural, seventy-two metres long, with Sydney-based artist Georgia Hill that gave me the confidence to know how to approach, design and deliver works on a mammoth scale. It was my previous work with James Cochran, aka Jimmy C, that gave me the confidence to fly halfway around the world by myself to create a wall with him in France, my first opportunity to take my public art practice overseas. The list is absolutely endless, and inspiration is everywhere; we need only to pause to take notice.

Activity
Design a mural for the front of your school or house.

Materials
Pencil and paper, acetate and a projector

Level
Medium

People
One or a group

Step 1

Take a photo of the front of your school or house.

Step 2

Print out the image twice and place an acetate sheet over the top of one of them and trace the building outlines. Now do the same on the other one but use tracing paper.

Step 3

On the tracing paper, design your mural. Complete this one.

Step 4

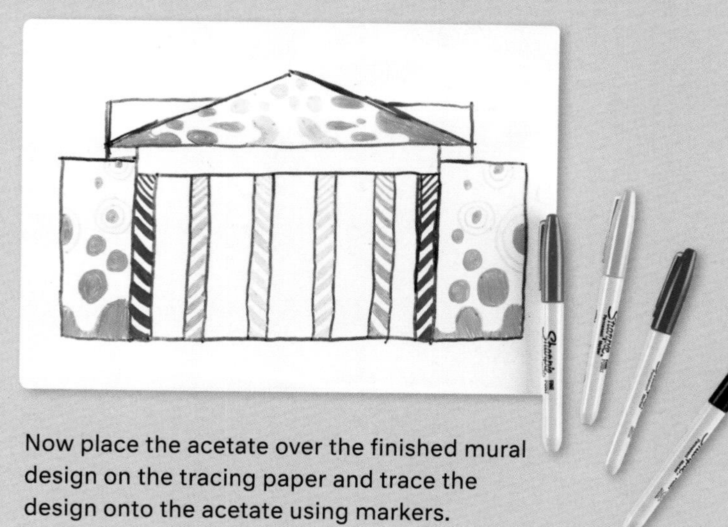

Now place the acetate over the finished mural design on the tracing paper and trace the design onto the acetate using markers.

Step 5

With both designs finished, play with scale by using the acetate design on an overhead projector and project it onto the building from the original image to see how the mural would look.

Brian Robinson

Kala Lagaw Ya / Wuthathi people, Cape York Peninsula, Torres Strait Islands, Queensland
born Waiben (Thursday Island), Queensland, 1973

Biography

Torres Strait Islander artist Brian Robinson lives and works in Cairns, Queensland. He is well known for his printmaking, sculpture and public art practice. Drawing on his Kala Lagaw Ya / Wuthathi heritage, his works merge Zenadh Kes (Torres Strait Islander) customs and traditions with contemporary pop culture references such as comics and movies. This combination of sources expresses the duality found in contemporary daily Zenadh Kes life, creating an accessible and relevant connection to culture for the upcoming generations.

Whether working in a large-scale format, or more intimately with the print medium, Robinson's practice importantly covers explorations into the natural environment, including land, sea and sky, and communicating the Zenadh Kes knowledge of and relationship to it. Significant animals, plants and stars are depicted in his work, together with contemporary subjects. Although these combinations may appear at times to be contradictory, it is Robinson's personal history and that of the collective Zenadh Kes people that he conveys in his works of art.

What made you become an artist?

I often say that I was born with a pencil in my hand because I was always drawing on scraps on paper, cardboard, kitchen walls, bedroom walls – no surface was sacred to me. I would create things using whatever I could find – recycled materials, cardboard boxes, old bike frames, as well as flotsam and jetsam from the surrounding shoreline.

Just like any other kid growing up on Waiben, the entire island was my playground. We were always out fishing, diving, hunting and playing sport, climbing trees, swimming at the wharf, getting up to mischief – seminal experiences growing up on a small island, surrounded by the sea.

Even though I grew up on an island in Torres Strait, I was still influenced by television and by comic books and other publications. I used to sit at the kitchen table at home and my grandparents' place for hours on end, drawing images from my imagination, from my memories, from comic books and from encyclopedias – anything I could get my hands on really, and that creative energy kept going.

When I rode around the island, my sketchbook and pencil followed, often accompanied by a basketball firmly wedged into the bike's frame. At the end of high school, I decided to go to art college, so I packed up my belongings, tucked my art portfolio under my arm and off I went to explore the art world as a full-time visual arts student.

There is an excitement that builds when creating art, but I've always enjoyed unravelling global artistic influences across the history of art. This curiosity led me along the path of curatorial practice as well, which gave me the ability to absorb greater knowledge of the arts industry.

detail: Brian Robinson, Kala Lagaw Ya/ Wuthathi people, Cape York Peninsula, Torres Strait Islands, Queensland, born Waiben (Thursday Island), Queensland 1973, *Empyreal: A Place and a Path in the Sky and on the Earth*, 2019, Cairns, Queensland, mixed media, dimensions variable; Acquisition through Tarnanthi: Festival of Contemporary Aboriginal & Torres Strait Islander Art supported by BHP 2020 © Brian Robinson

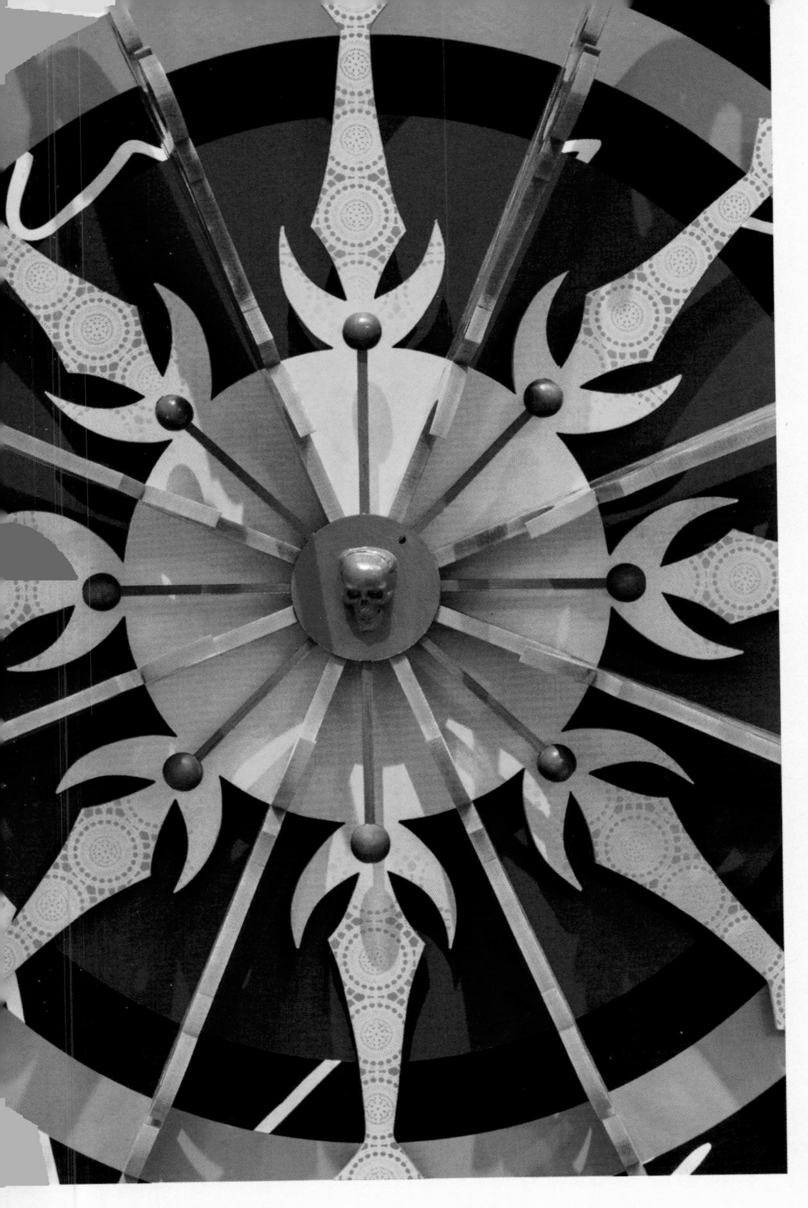

How would you describe your work?

I am a visual contemporary storyteller. I am known for my printmaking, sculpture and public art, in which I use a variety of techniques to produce kaleidoscopic works that are bold, innovative and distinctive, underpinned by intriguing narratives revealing the strong tradition of storytelling from my island home.

Like the ocean currents that course through the Torres Strait, a myriad of cultural influences runs through my family's ancestry and my own lived experience. My family are fisher folk, whose Roman Catholic faith exists in synergy with traditional spirituality. My images are often strange and seemingly incongruous concoctions, yet there are many recurring motifs and characters that appear – co-opted into the spirit realm of the islander imagination.

My art reflects the tropical marine environment – the land, the sea, the sky and the stars, and the inhabitants of those environments. It is an essential part of my life and my culture, a culture that is imbued with the customs and traditions of the Maluyligal people of Torres Strait, the Wuthathi people of Cape York Peninsula and the Dayak people of Borneo. The animals from ancestral narratives and their presence today are also an integral feature of my intoxicating work.

What is the role of an artist?

Art is one of the most powerful tools of communication on earth. Not only do the visual arts provide pleasure and creative inspiration, they also help to foster dialogue and bring important issues to light. Artists have a strong influence on the development of society because art brings communities and people together to create shared visions for the future as well as document history.

My role as an Indigenous artist is to create works of art that talk about my experiences, my cultural values and heritage, and my connection to my family's ancestral lands and the environment. This is done through the mediums of drawing, printmaking, sculpture, painting and public art.

Maintaining this connection is vital for passing on important cultural stories and customs to younger generations. As a visual person, I see the obvious beauty and dimensions of the world around me, as others do, but I also see a mythical landscape, which at the same time is woven together with this world.

Creation ancestors form part of that mythical landscape, and creative practices such visual art, performing arts and literature are ways by which this connection and relationship are expressed. Artists have an important place in contemporary Indigenous life.

detail: Brian Robinson, Kala Lagaw Ya/ Wuthathi people, Cape York Peninsula, Torres Strait Islands, Queensland, born Waiben (Thursday Island), Queensland 1973, *Empyreal: A Place and a Path in the Sky and on the Earth*, 2019, Cairns, Queensland, mixed media, dimensions variable; Acquisition through Tarnanthi: Festival of Contemporary Aboriginal & Torres Strait Islander Art supported by BHP 2020 © Brian Robinson

What do you enjoy about making art?

Thinking big and dreaming are essential for nurturing creativity. The energy and enjoyment that come from having the ability to physically create a work of art that has emerged from my bizarre imagination and my curiosity about the world have been my motivation to art-making since I was a child.

Art brings out the child in us all. I love playing with ink, paint, paper, glue, wood, screws, plastic, jigsaw, sander, and the list goes on – the things that have become the tools of choice for my artistic career.

Who inspired you?

Inspiration for my practice comes from a multitude of visual sources and amazing people. The first inspiring people that I know and cherish is my family – my loving wife Tanya, my daughter Amber, and my sons Raidon and Leonardo. The support, humour, and mountains of toys and other visual paraphernalia they provide are the foundation for my artistic life. The boundless energy and curiosity they possess are often mirrored and intertwined throughout the works of art I create.

Others I turn to in search of inspirational work are the Italian Renaissance masters Michelangelo and Leonardo, German painter and printmaker Albrecht Dürer, Dutch graphic artist M.C. Escher, children's book author and illustrator Theodore Seuss Geisel, aka Dr Seuss, and fellow Torres Strait Islander artists, the late Allson Edrick Tabuai and Dr Ken Thaiday senior, to mention a few.

Last but definitely not least, my past ancestral family have provided me with inspirational narratives and amazing artforms, which I weave throughout my work of art. These stories and objects often form the basis from which I create – twisting and turning, pulling and pushing until the new work is complete.

detail: Brian Robinson, Kala Lagaw Ya/Wuthathi people, Cape York Peninsula, Torres Strait Islands, Queensland, born Waiben (Thursday Island), Queensland 1973, *Empyreal: A Place and a Path in the Sky and on the Earth*, 2019, Cairns, Queensland, mixed media, dimensions variable; Acquisition through Tarnanthi: Festival of Contemporary Aboriginal & Torres Strait Islander Art supported by BHP 2020 © Brian Robinson

Installation view: Brian Robinson, *Empyreal: A Place and a Path in the Sky and on the Earth*, 2019, Tarnanthi: Festival of Contemporary Aboriginal & Torres Strait Islander Art, Art Gallery of South Australia

Gallery of South Australia stands
Kaurna land. We recognise Kaurna
ople as the custodians of the Adelaide
ins. We also recognise the Indigenous
stodians from other parts of Australia
d from overseas.

Activity

Create a drawing incorporating your favourite patterns and a pop culture reference from your childhood. It might be a character from your favourite TV show, comic book or movie, or your favourite soft drink or chocolate bar. Mix them together for a surprising result. Here are some examples to help you get started.

Materials
Pencil or pen, paper

Level
Easy

People
One or two

Step 1

Think of your favourite types of patterns and draw them on a sheet of paper; use this sheet to brainstorm.

Step 2

Now, using a separate sheet of paper, write down or draw some of your favourite pop culture references or characters from your childhood.

Tip

You may want to add characters such as Mickey Mouse, Bart Simpson or Jack Skellington.

Step 3

On a fresh sheet of paper, select your favourite reference and pattern and combine them together to create your work of art.

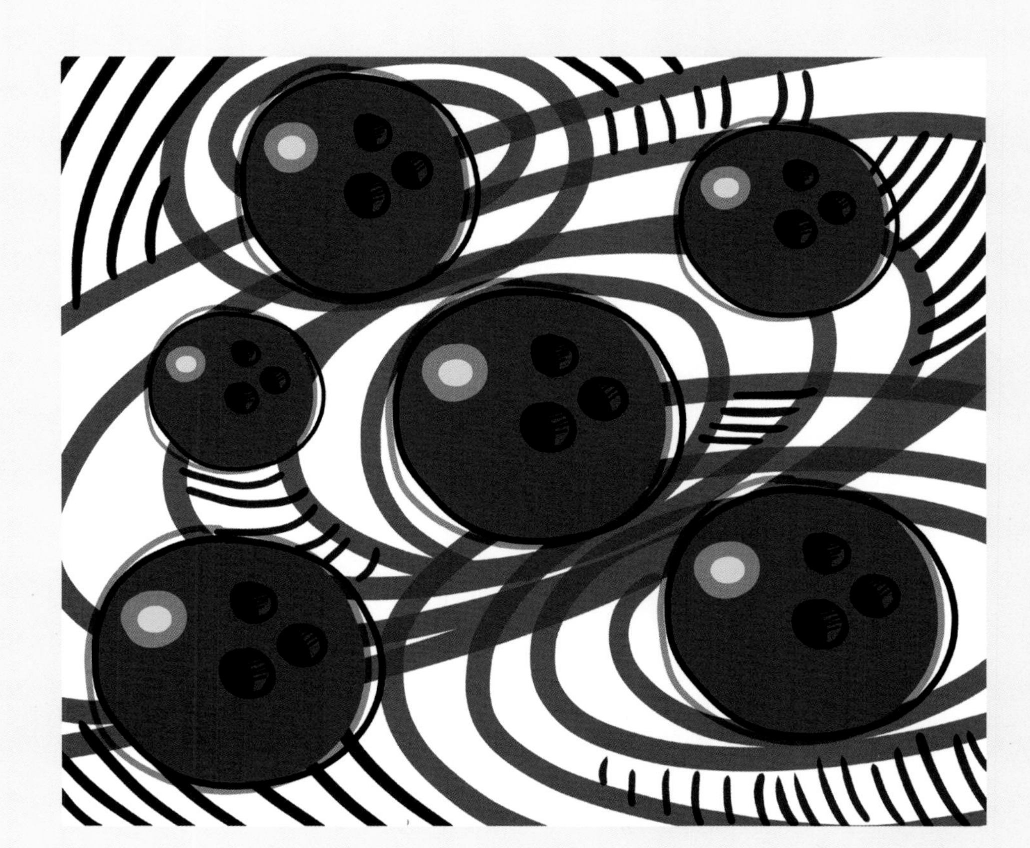

Tips

Try using the pattern inside the character, outside the character or repeat the character to create a pattern.

Noŋgirrŋa Marawili

Madarrpa clan, Yolŋu people, Northern Territory
born Darrpirra, Northern Territory, c.1938

Step 4

Complete your auto-portrait and take it for a spin!

Betty Muffler

Pitjantjatjara people, South Australia

born near Watarru, South Australia, 1944

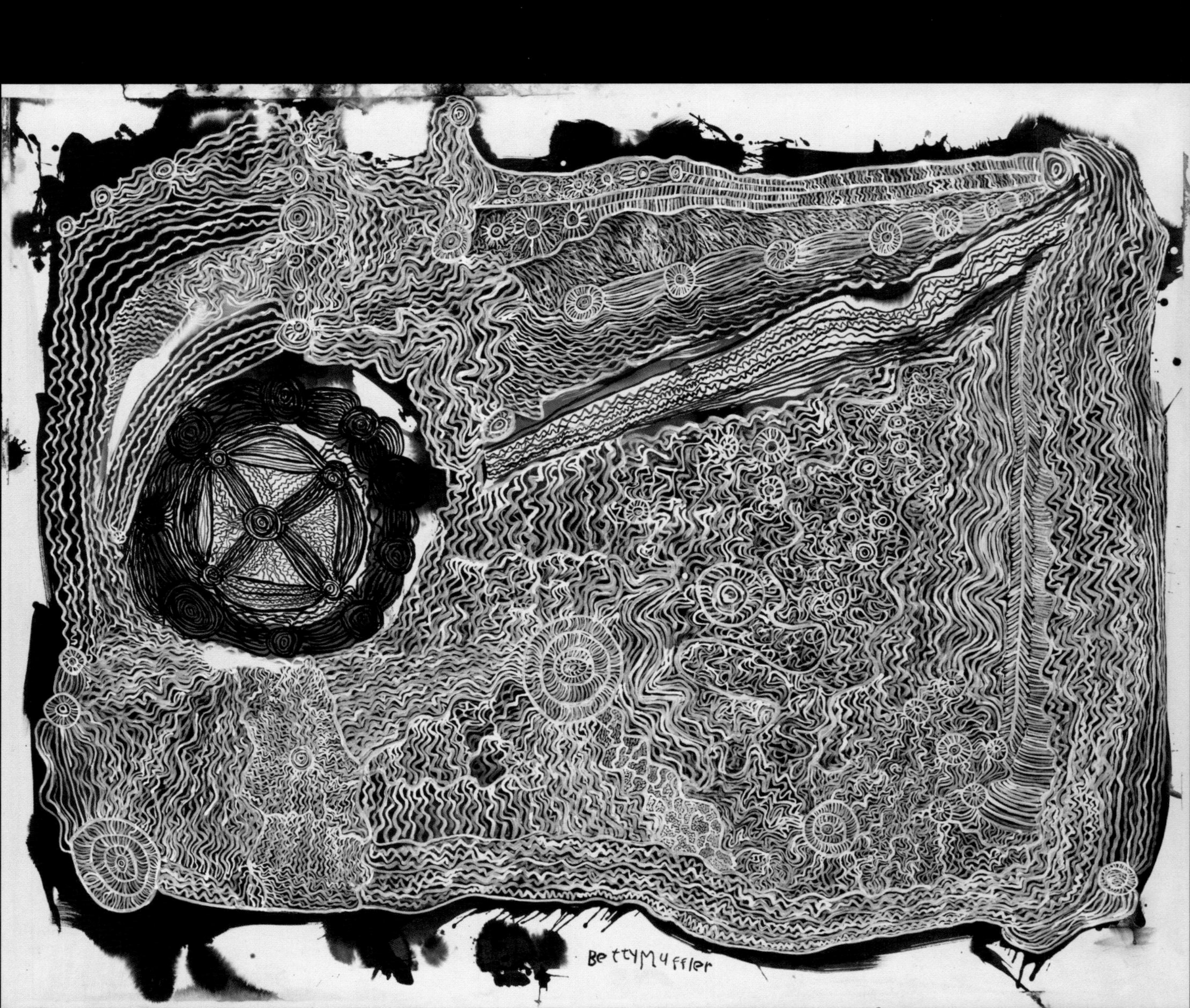

Biography

Senior artist Betty Muffler was born on Country near Watarru, which lies close to the border between South Australia and Western Australia. She grew up in Pukatja (Ernabella) after being displaced from her family, who passed away as a result of the devastating effects of the British nuclear testing that occurred near Maralinga in the 1950s and 1960s.

Muffler is not only an artist, but also a cultural leader and *ngangkari* (traditional healer). She works with the Ngaanyatjarra Pitjantjatjara Yankunytjatjara (NPY) Women's Council and medical practitioners to support and assist Aṉangu health and wellbeing. Her work as a *ngangkari* is expressed in her paintings, which often show important sites on Country, sites that are also places of healing and good energy. Her paintings are characterised by their limited palette, as Muffler frequently uses only one colour to create her works. Muffler paints wavy lines in tight formations to depict and capture the intense energy and healing powers found at these important sites.

She currently works from Iwantja Arts in Indulkana on the Aṉangu Pitjantjatjara Yankunytjatjara (APY) Lands, where she also creates woven *tjanpi* (native grass) works, drawings and prints alongside her paintings.

What made you become an artist?

I started painting so I could share my knowledge and experience with other people.

How would you describe your work?

My paintings are about *ngangkari* (traditional healing), what it feels like and what it means to be *ngangkari* – so they're really important to me. They're all about my feelings and my thoughts about my *ngangkari* work. I love painting – thinking and feeling and moving around the canvas, following my thoughts and ideas. I don't use a lot of colours, just one really; that's my way: colour *kutju* (one colour).

What is the role of an artist?

I think that my work as an artist is similar to the work I do as a *ngangkari* – helping people to feel better. I really like my *ngangkari* work and working on my painting at the art centre. It makes me happy to know that I'm helping people to feel good – I know it's a really important job.

What do you enjoy about making art?

I love making art because it makes me feel happy, calm and peaceful. The movement I try to show in my drawings is like the energy that flows through people and places – it's invisible to most people but *ngangkari* like me can see spirits and feel a lot of different energy. When I'm painting or drawing, I'm feeling the good energy; it's connecting with my spirit and all of these feelings become part of the work of art.

Who inspired you?

I'm inspired by my family. My sisters are all great artists too. We all do different ways: drawing, painting, *tjanpi* (native grass) weaving.

Betty Muffler, Pitjantjatjara people, South Australia, born near Watarru, South Australia 1944, *Ngangkaṟi Ngura (Healing Country)*, 2020, Indulkana, South Australia, pigmented ink on paper, 122.0 x 152.0 cm

photo: Grant Hancock

Activity

Create a collaborative drawing with a friend or two.
Create your own mark and repeat it; is it a soft mark or harsh mark?
Does it complement your friends' marks?

Materials

Pencils + large paper

Step 1

Roll out a large piece of paper and discuss with friends what mark-marking you would like to use. Think about your personality; how can you describe it with a pencil mark? Is it quiet and soft, or loud and bold?

detail: Betty Muffler, Pitjantjatjara people, South Australia, born near Watarru, South Australia 1944, *Ngangkaṟi Ngura (Healing Country)*, 2020, Indulkana, South Australia, pigmented ink on paper, 122.0 x 152.0 cm

photo: Grant Hancock

Step 2

Once you have decided on your marks, get started on your collaborative work of art.

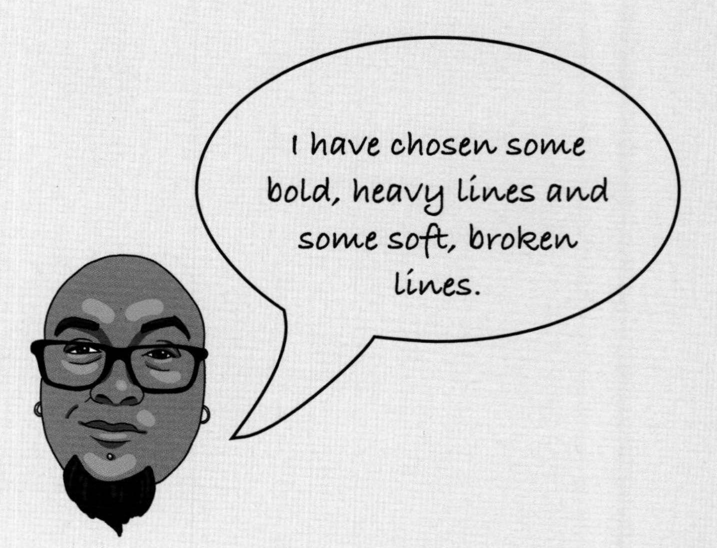

Step 3

As you are all making your marks, think about how your marks can complement the marks your friends are making.

Grace Lillian Lee

Meriam Mir people, Erub (Darnley) Island, Torres Strait Islands, Queensland
born Cairns, Queensland, 1988

Biography

Grace Lillian Lee is an artist who draws on her diverse heritage to inform her art-making, which includes creating wearable works of art. These works are often referred to as sculptures, as they blur the typical boundaries between fashion and art.

Lee studied fashion design at RMIT University, in Melbourne, but was taught the 'prawn or grasshopper weaving' technique by the renowned artist Uncle Ken Thaiday, from Erub (Darnley) Island. This technique is the same as that adopted by Torres Strait Islander artists to create the woven animals that are used as decorative ornaments and children's toys. However, rather than weaving with traditional materials such as coconut leaf, banana fibre or pandanus, Lee uses processed fibres like cotton webbing and yarn, often in bright colours, to create her forms. At times she weaves in feathers, beads and coral.

In her works, Lee explores ideas of identity and body adornment across cultures. Combining cultural craftsmanship with expressions of contemporary trends in fashion and design, Lee creates new and innovative works, which explore ongoing connections to culture and identity.

Beyond her role as an artist, she also engages and collaborates with Aboriginal and Torres Strait Islander communities, encouraging the younger generations to voice their creative expressions in the fashion and design realms.

What made you become an artist?

My father is an artist and a fitter and turner and my mother is a hairdresser. So, for as long as I can remember, I was always very inspired by their collective creativity. When I had the opportunity to visit my father's family on Thursday Island, for my great-grandmother's tombstone unveiling, I was introduced to traditional ways, including cooking, dancing and art. This experience opened my mind and ignited a desire to learn more about my cultural background. The best way I knew how to respond to this was through fashion design.

How would you describe your work?

I like to describe my practice as a place where art meets fashion and culture.

It's an exploration and celebration of my cultural lineage, where I can explore fabrications, space and form on the body.

What do you enjoy about making art?

I enjoy having the opportunity to share my practice with the wider community, while also reconnecting and learning more about my culture.

Who inspired you?

Uncle Ken Thaiday has been a mentor of mine since the beginning of my career. He was the first person to teach me how to weave, so I attribute my success to him.

Model wearing a selection of neckpieces by Grace Lillian Lee, from the 2015 Tarnanthi exhibition *Shimmer*
photo: Carly K. Photography

Activity
'Get your weave on'

Materials
Strips of coloured card

Level
Medium

People
One

Step 1

Make a 'V' shape by placing one strip over the other, secure them into place with glue, tape or stapler.

Step 2

Fold the strip on the bottom over the strip on the top.

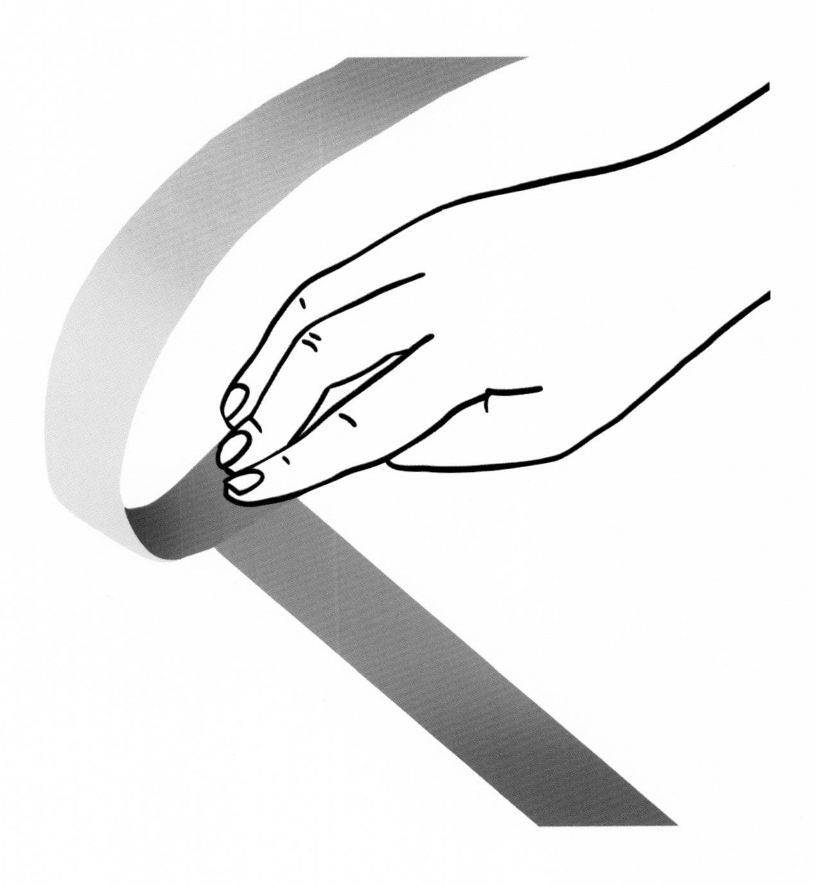

Step 3

Again, fold the bottom strip over the top strip. Repeat until you run out of paper to fold.

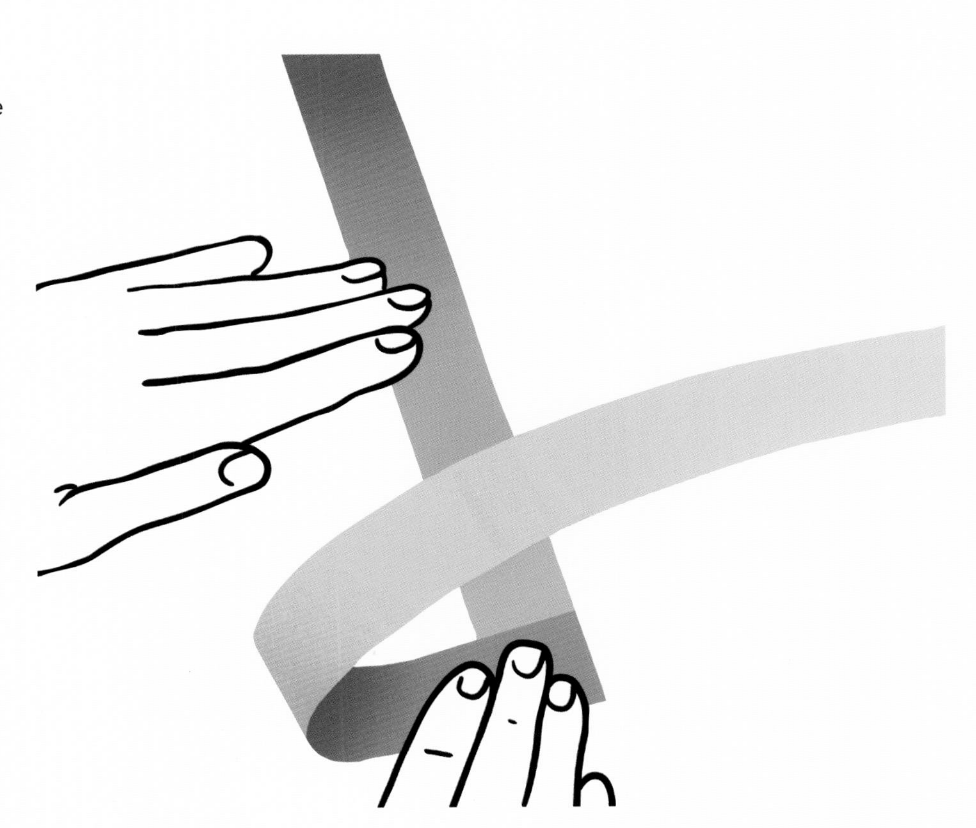

Grace Lillian Lee, Meriam Mir people, Erub (Darnley) Island, Torres Strait Islands, Queensland, born Cairns, Queensland 1988, *Intertwined*, 2015, Cairns, Queensland, cotton, 43.0 x 38.0 cm; Acquisition through Tarnanthi: Festival of Contemporary Aboriginal and Torres Strait Islander Art supported by BHP 2016

Step 4

When you have finished you will have a cube of folded paper.

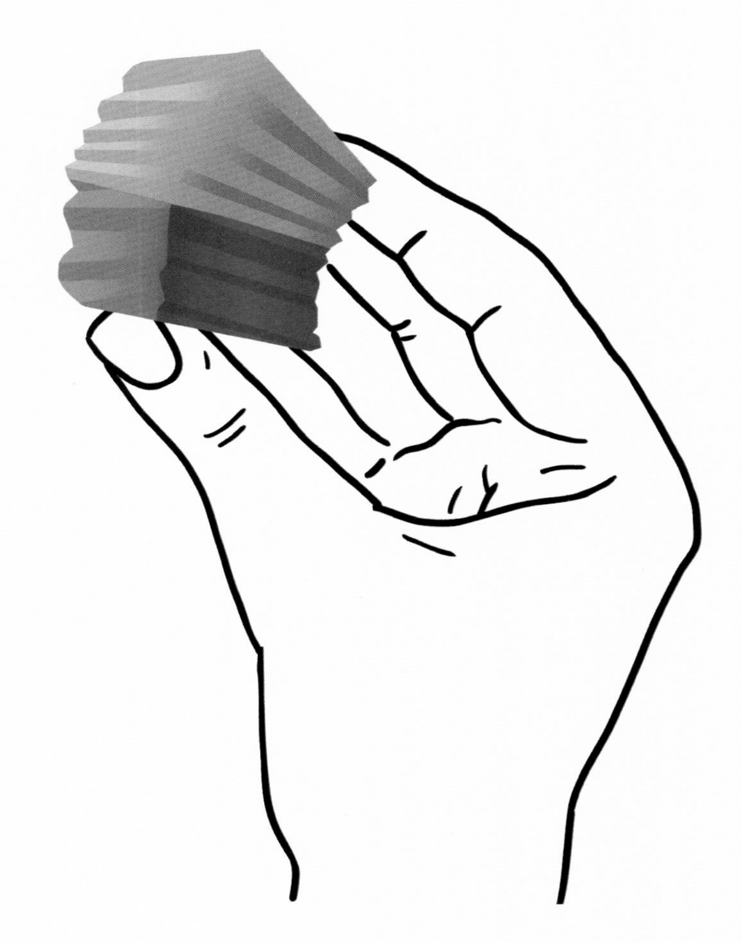

Step 5

Take the top and bottom folds of the cube and pull them apart to see the weave you have created.

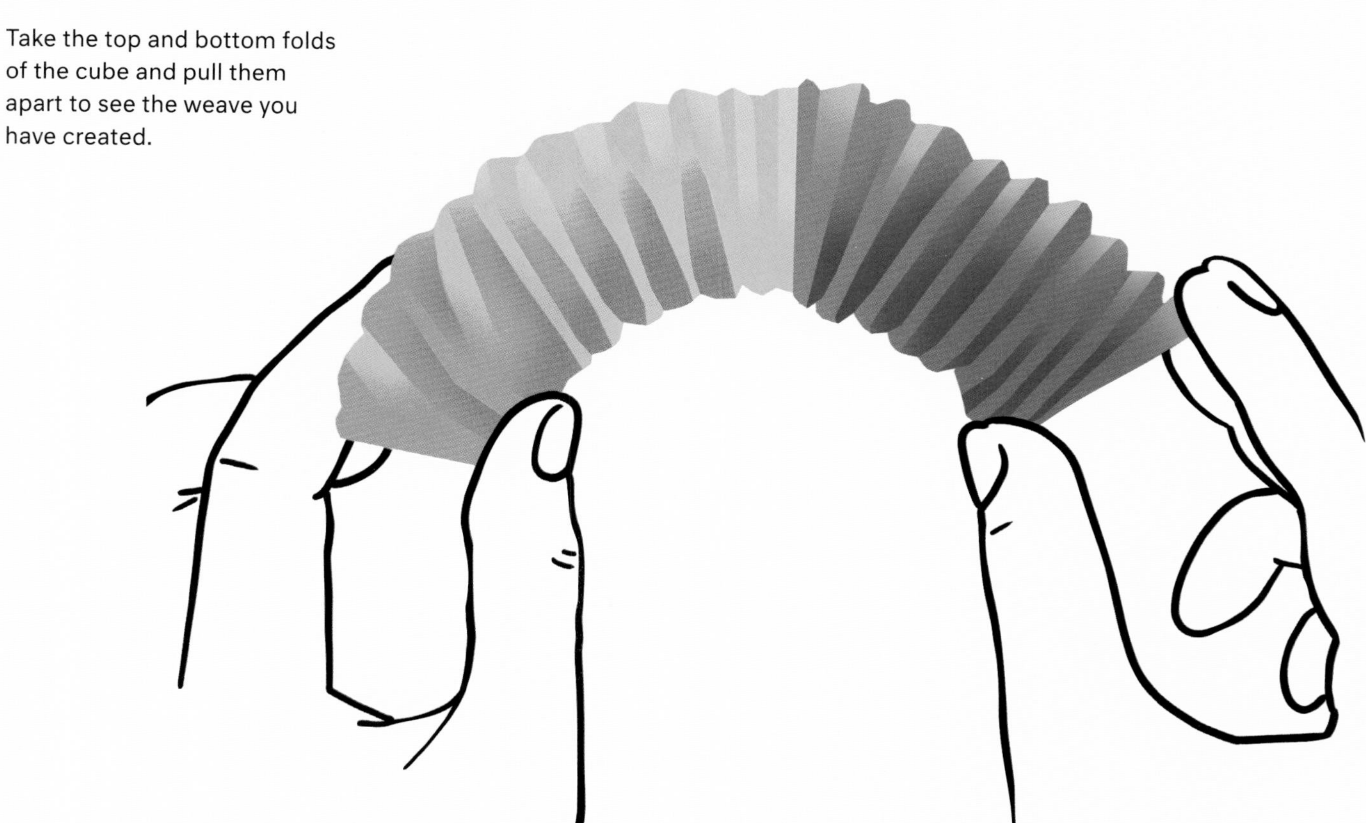

April Phillips

Wiradjuri people, New South Wales
born Sydney, Gadigal Country, 1983

Biography

April Phillips is a Wiradjuri–Scottish woman of the Galari peoples. Her arts practice is cemented in digital arts, illustration, and AR (augmented reality) research. April leans into character design as a narrative tool to explore empathy, fun and form. Her use of vivid colour and unlikely digital processes celebrates the potential of computer art for a new world.

April is a dedicated mentor to many young people in assisting them to build concepts and technical skills in digital art-making.

What made you become an artist?

Making art feels good; it's so fun to see an idea come to life. Sometimes this happens when we imagine, sometimes it's all about playing with materials or techniques as we build skills. I make art on computers, iPads and on virtual reality headsets. Technology is fun and a big part of my art practice.

How would you describe your work?

My work is vivid, fun, weird and takes us to places we haven't been but want to go! I work on machines and that makes my work a bit futuristic.

What is the role of an artist?

Artists need to speak strong with our words but, most importantly, be strong in our art. Sometimes what we say is quiet, or little; sometimes what we speak is big and loud. The role of the artist is to put that strength into our art. Being an artist is finding the truth-telling space in your tummy, when your tummy says 'yes it's done or on the good path'.

What do you enjoy about making art?

The best thing about making art is the process. If something isn't working, keep going; make a different version, another one, or try another colour, process, material or way of thinking. All of the works of art we love are the result of testing, so don't give up! It makes me so happy to feel as if the hard work led me to a work of art. It's like an adventure to make a work of art and that's what I enjoy most.

Who inspired you?

I have had some generous teachers at school, as well as friends who have taught me skills and made my mind sparkle with inspiration. Sometimes people think art isn't a 'real' job and they tried to stop me – those people inspired me too because I wanted to prove them wrong!

Activity
Design a billboard and cardboard village

Materials
Cardboard boxes, and tubes, glue and tape
Acrylic paint, textas, pens and coloured paper
Optional: device to create digital artwork
Toys, fabric and other props for world building

Level
Medium to hard

People
Three to six

April would like to thank the young artists and supporting educators of Bermagui pre-school, and Meadow Leclerc + Élodie Leclerc who created the boxes featured.

Step 1

Close your eyes and imagine an ideal world, a place where you, your friends and family can live your best life. In this world there will be no advertising on billboards, only art and positive messages. Brainstorm some ideas for billboards, based on the things you notice, your interests and passions and any issues you believe in.

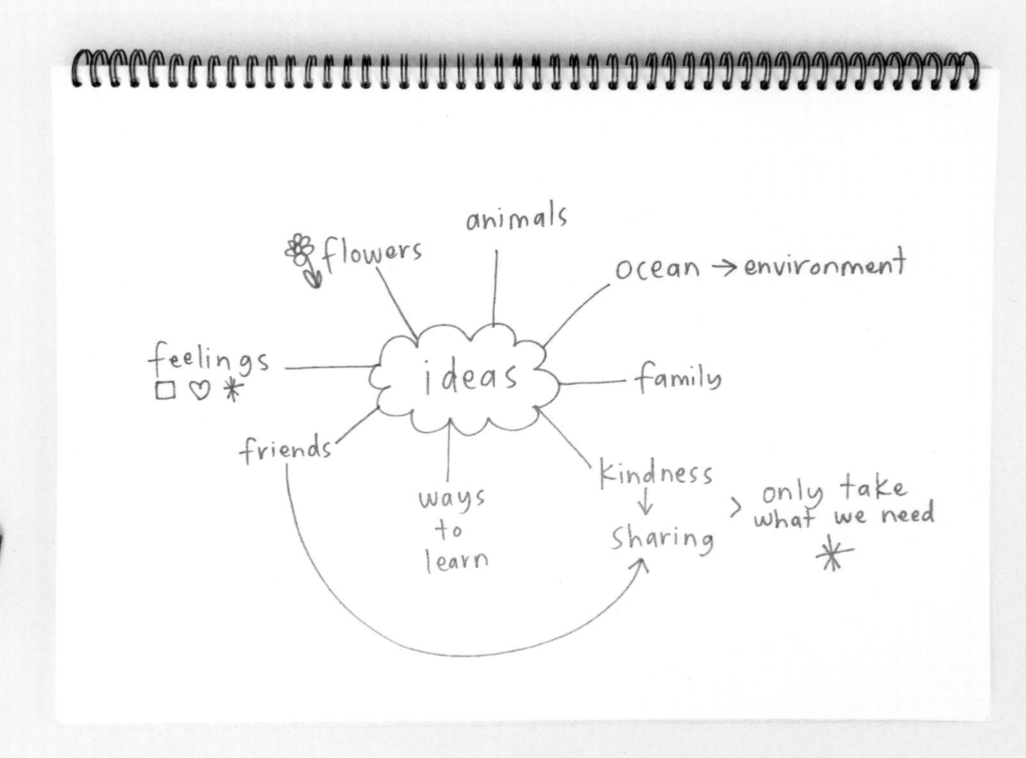

Step 2

Create some billboard designs using a long narrow format. If you are drawing on a digital device, try 1232 px wide and 308 px high, and then print in full colour. If you are drawing on paper, use the long side and fold and cut it so it becomes a long thin rectangle. Use a combination of image and text to deliver your message.

Step 3

Paint boxes and tubes to become houses, museums, galleries, shops and community centres. Try using a combination of paint, coloured paper and drawing tools.

Step 4

Print digital billboards and glue to a backing board. Attach the billboards to the buildings with tape.

Step 5

Arrange the buildings in your world with trees, people and water. Use fabric, blankets and other materials to add colour and texture to the scene. Make some people and add some toys to bring your world to life.

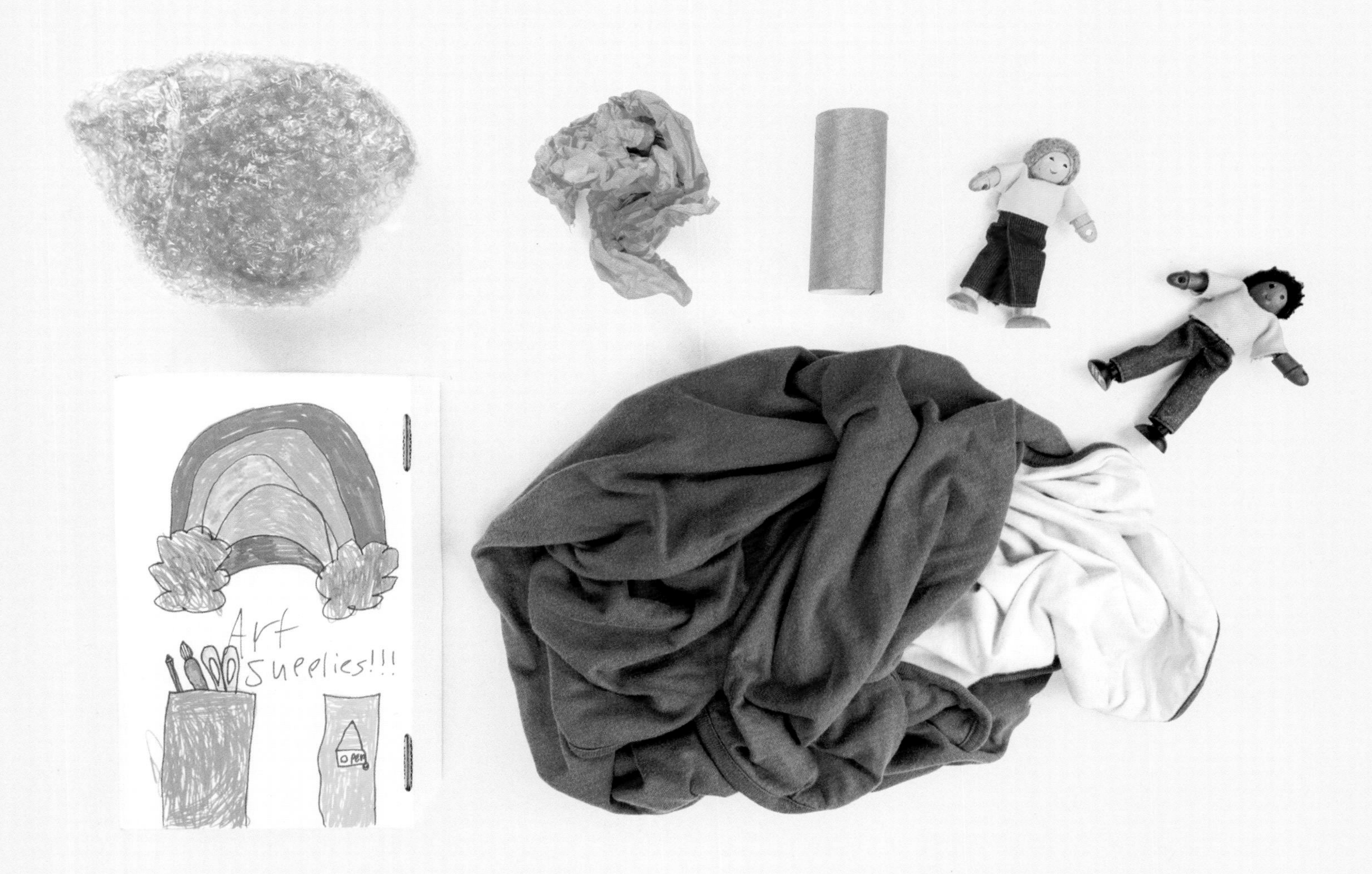

The artists

John Prince Siddon

photo: Susie Blatchford/Pixel Poetry

Painting (acrylic), sculpture

Elizabeth Yanyi Close

photo: Renee Readett Creative

Painting, public art

Brian Robinson

photo: Saul Steed

Printmaking, sculpture, public art

Noŋgirrŋa Marawili

photo: Nat Rogers

Painting (earth pigments, recycled print toner pigment on bark), printmaking

Marlene Rubuntja

Marlene Rubuntja teaching her granddaughter Rhonda; Courtesy the artist and Yarrenyty Arltere Artists

Sculpture (textile, fabric), painting

Reko Rennie

photo: David Varga

Painting, video, installation, sculpture, public art

Betty Muffler

photo: Rhett Hammerton

Painting (acrylic and ink on linen) drawing, printmaking

Grace Lillian Lee

Sculpture, textiles, weaving

April Phillips

Illustration, digital drawing, sculpture

AGSA

Make & Create was published by the Art Gallery of South Australia, November 2021

Book and illustrations: Thomas Readett
Contributions: Kylie Neagle and Gloria Strzelecki
Design and production: Antonietta Itropico
Prepress: Darren Dunne
Printed in Adelaide by Graphic Print Group, Adelaide

Distributed in Australia by Thames & Hudson
Portside Business Park, 11 Central Boulevard, Fisherman's Bend, Victoria 3207

ISBN: 978-1-921668-50-0

Art Gallery of South Australia
North Terrace, Adelaide SA 5000
artgallery.sa.gov.au

Tarnanthi is presented in partnership with BHP and with the support of the Government of South Australia